Butterfly Poetry
Butterfly Poet

by

Leona Peace

DORRANCE
PUBLISHING CO
EST. 1920
PITTSBURGH, PENNSYLVANIA 15238

Dorrance Publishing Co
585 Alpha Drive
Suite 103
Pittsburgh, PA 15238
Visit our website at www. dorrancebookstore.com

ISBN: 979-8-89127-618-5
eISBN: 979-8-89127-116-6

Monkeys

I see monkeys in the tree trying to grab the elephants, wee wee wee! The elephants started throwing apples at the monkeys. The monkeys said, "Can't we all just be friends. Let's watch a movie together."

The elephants hollered, "Creepy spiders!" The elephants told the monkeys to stop monkeying around. The monkeys kicked the elephants in the treehouse. As they hollered, "Creepy spiders!" Now all the birds flew out, scaring the monkeys off. The elephants hollering, "Creepy spiders, creepy spiders!" I guess they couldn't all be friends.

Adventures

Dinosaurs walked this earth one hundred sixty-five million years ago; some carried purses, most of them cursed. A lot of them stole to survive. They mostly ate vegetables. Some of them were tall but a lot of them were short. My mother told me a story of how she saw dinosaurs fighting giraffes. They fought so hard they dug a hole in the ground. Oh no, there are babies being born. Here come elephants. Now we got dinosaurs, giraffes, and elephants talking at the same time; it's chaos down here. The elephants said they have a plan to get back to solid ground. The elephants piggybacked to get all to the top. The giraffe pulled the elephant's legs as they used his trunks to get the last one up. The giraffe told the elephant he got the gift of the gab. They all laughed, then fell back down the hole. You heard all hollering, "Oh nooo!" The elephants said, "Momma told us not to play 'til the job's done." So the elephants did the same routine again, only this time they won. The giraffe said, "About time. Dinosaurs went extinct sixty-five million years ago."

Mysteries

Y'all want to hear something funny. As I walked out the door this morning to go to work I noticed somebody stole one of my reindeers I paid three hundred dollars for. I called the Abington police; they took a report. I said, "Everybody in the whole complex is getting investigated." I got so loud that the neighbors came out to find out what was wrong. The neighbor told the officers they saw the same display upstairs. I said, "Everybody's getting investigated."

The cop said, "I came out to do a report about this one reindeer." Here comes Santa walking down the hall, talking about, "Ho ho ho, did you get all you asked for for Christmas."

I said, "Somebody stole my reindeers and I want them back."

The officer said, "I thought you said it was one." He said, "Mrs., I'ma half to check inside your home."

I said, "Okay, not without a warrant." He went in anyway just to find the reindeer behind the door.

He said, "Hands behind you back, please, for a false report."

My next door neighbors said, "Oh, come on it's Christmas."

The officer said, "Okay, you get a pass."

I wiped my forehead and said, "Luckily for him 'cause I was about to make a citizen's arrest for no warrant."

The officer said, "All this over a reindeer that wasn't even stolen."

Matters

Matters of the heart that weigh us down. Turn it over to the Lord like the lost and found. My body is here but my mind's somewhere else. You gotta eat healthy or it's bad for your health. I'ma paint my car like the rainbow, so when you see me passing through you think about God, and when he comes back, don't cry, you tried. Don't mess around and get the mark of the beast. Father, I'm guilty. I've been doing the least. I'm talkin' about biblical. I'm talkin' about reality. I drink my source then I talk it up. They say that's last but God's walking. What matter of the heart that weighs us down. Turn it over to the Lord like the lost and found.

Shadows

Some things are arbitrary in life, uncontrolled or unrestricted. Should have been Bernie Madoff who messed many folks over. The middle class is what kept the economy going. Got me wondering how we are growing; looks like where going back to the recession. People stressing about the prices. We're in a crisis; my life is not where my life should be. 401s in place; will it be there or be erased? Some things are arbitrary in life, uncontrolled or unrestricted. Listen, but we don't listen. Where is the piece to the puzzle? This has left us all puzzled. We need better investments. My guess, the question will be when and how, while we wild out, wild out a day late and a dollar short.

No Vision

You want it black. See, they're trying to treat me like I'm coffee 'cause I'm light. See, no time for small-minded people; they're blind, they can't see, no vision to begin with, so why pretend then? Black power. We are not going to talk about white prejudice or black prejudice 'cause it comes in many forms. I'm the storm you should have been warned of. I'ma do you like psychic proof; be gone lies being told, stolen like you down to be. Black and proud to be white and proud to be Chinese and proud to be Jamaican and proud to be Spanish and proud to be. I just want to bring out the best in we.

Humor

You ever met someone that has a since of humor, then I can show you someone who has a tumor. They mark you 'cause it's funny. The spark be when it's sunny; sense of humor to keep as growing. Sometimes not knowing how we offend in then the sense of harm begins if we don't mark 'em there's know spark then. Know meaning they know we slow in salted because we fault it. Who brought it, not cash, but at last they live to be although they can't see at times to pretend to be kind; not why you feel like. I just bide my time; time will adjust to humor the earth; be known tumor humor k-n-o-w once again the pain runs deep; if I pick up the dirt then we won't know who's hurting. I know I'm lazy. I pray to God every day that he saves me. The earth is full of enjoyment but until I'm anointed I find enjoyment in the pleasures of life. He died and came twice; you ever meet someone who has a sense of humor? Then I can show you someone who has a tumor; the humor is.

Easter

I see this rabbit. I gotta hippity hop; it's about to be Easter. My Lord has risen; people all over the world and even in prison feel lifted knowing we are all gifted; although life has its ups and down, we gotta believe; open up your hearts; as long as we have his love within us you're gonna always understand to begin within. Jesus gave us this world to cherish. Welcome him with open arms. I see this rabbit. I got to hippity hop' it's about to be Easter. He gives to us the brave; we must trust that he will be back again someday, one day; until then I'ma reminisce about the love he gave us. the brave us/ I see this rabbit. I got to hippity hop.

Needle

Feeling like a needle in the haystack until you black out, come back to deal with the reality; that's not fact, Couples doing drugs together, feelings loved forever, so you chasing that needle like a dream. They feelin' with the shakes that breaks families apart; most start with the loss of hopefulness, motionless, coasting trips, can't get the monkey off your back, feeling like a needle in a haystack; drugs overpower you, useless, taking the shower, shoot like mostly you see in the movies. Don't move me. Sometimes you got to trust like some medicines we take and cuff drugs. I don't need you steady, trying to believe you, believe you. I don't need shit; you might as well call me Stevie Wonder 'cause I don't see shit; they say drugs put me out, like I'm fine with that; now my mind is whack, feeling like a needle in the haystack.

*Y*our problem is you think you're special. I am God's creation, my imagination, my thinking. I won't let your insecurities bother me. I am special in many ways; you just can't see when I'm in the middle of the road and don't know which way to go. I'm still special. I bless the Lord for making me who I am, teaching me the way to be, leading me so I can see I am special beyond, my beauty beyond what the eyes can see. I am special because of me, special in so many ways. I've chosen to be special for the world to see; special, that's me.

heard you was a hoe. I don't give a crap 'cause I was plottin' to let you go. I'ma keep it on the low, low, you slow for what you thought you knew; leave a nigga clueless; fuck a blueprint; bring it red. I'm dealing with the shade; they ain't said shit yet until it's really wet in the pussy; that's when it drop shit. I'm not a fuckin' thot bitch, waiting for a drop hit. I'm out trying to clock shit, when all I hear is hot shit, not talking about your lyrics, pal pal pal; they don't fear it. I heard you was a hoe. I don't give a crap 'cause I was plotting to let you go.

Magic

If I told you I can do magic, would you believe me? I'm nothing like the magic carpet, you can't walk on me, you got to talk to me. I'm nothing like a glance. I'm your only chance. I'm like a one-way street, is only one way in and no way out; if I told you I can do magic would you believe me? I speak specifics; when it leaks they get it watch it evaporate. You got to concentrate; if I told you I can do magic, would you believe me?

15

When darkness tries to roll over my boat I'ma keep rowing. I'm not afraid. When sorrows try to confuse me, broken and pain is all I know. I won't be frozen when my fears tries to consume me. I won't be captive. I won't be captivated. I'm not afraid to leave my past behind. When I no longer have a place to hide, when darkness tries to row over my boat, I'ma keep stroking. I'm not afraid to cry and keep going, when darkness tries to roll over my boat.

on't y'all put the guns down, you burn now, don't run now. Shot a nigga down like it was worth it, never took the time to care that it hurt. Bombarded by situations we allow to happen. The enemy is clapping with those messed-up facts that leave you snapping. Momma, Grandmomma, grieving on them, begging for one day to see the sun, to see them smile again. We wild and them. My son, my daughter, We can't run. I can't forget/ Tomorrow you're still the show; put the guns down. If you don't I'ma throw a shoe at you like the one that was thrown at Bush; can't we all live in peace? Peace.

Hustle

Y'all be trying to hustle for ass. When I hustle I'm bringing it first class; don't laugh, how I blast on 'em. Do the math on them. Top shape, ain't no faking them. I'm trying to escape the sun. When I run I bring them digits up. I keep that money coming in, so when a nigga wanna run, all he can do is grin. No pretend for what we sin to be. When I hustle I'm bringing it first class; don't laugh, how I blast on them. Do the math on them; they don't even talk like me, walk like me. I'ma boss you see. I don't play with them anymore, lay with 'em. I'm not that cat; I take my nine lives back. Y'all be trying to hustle for ass; when I hustle I'm bringing it first class. You got to understand what it means to be privileged.

*H*ow would you feel if I told you my life is in one wallet? How would you feel if I said you just don't try it? How would you feel if all I said are you crying? If you had one wish would you make it the wildest? How would you feel if I said you got to try it? How would you feel if all said is you lying, and nobody's buying it. Now you're crying. How would you feel? How would you feel if I said you had to leave? She said she would sneeze. Baby don't leave. I realize I need you. Baby, please, baby, please, how would you feel?

We can lessen the loneliness of not belonging when we look at the woman in the mirror, believing the challenges we face every day. We race the trace not to chase away, no double standards when representing ourselves, using our vulnerability as strengths, not dealing with the self-consciousness that wears us down; here's your crown. We can lessen the loneliness of not belonging.

Fame

Here's my story of fame, not fifteen minutes some would say. I'm not talking about the bedroom fame. Famous. I'm not talking about clothes neither, even though I admire their beautiful talent, their styles, don't know much about their manes. Fame has many forms and I'm just here to join the storm. I like knowing I'm going to be remembered forever, after feeling like I've been looked down on a pond. I want the kind of fame that comes with being nice, going out one's way to make others' lives in this world magnificent; just know I'm famous for making this world a better place for children and their children and so on not because all of the money I've made, but by the way I've chosen to live my life, famous for my formula. My momma said I was very talented, I thought she meant basketball. I would have never thought in my wildest dreams I would have been famous. I wasn't looking for it, famous found me. I couldn't seem to run from it, so I'm learning how to embrace it, balancing life. When I leave this world think about the stories I've left; you're the best suited; remember me. Famous.

Teach

They say we teach people how to treat you a lot of this. I'm about to say may not reach you; some of us go above and beyond like Celine Dion; very magnificent; as we watch we learn some that is everyone that watch don't learn 'til it turns and turn never got the picture; it was scribbled all over. They say we teach people how to treat you like when you stay in an abusive relationship, teach like when you accept abusive language, teaches. Do I have to keep being specific? They say we teach people how to treat you.

Frogs By the Pool

What if I told you frogs don't ribbit, they pivot; if I told you frogs talked to turtles would you laugh? Frogs are green, frogs are mean; here are the stories I've heard about frogs: I was told frogs are great swimmers, so I put them in the pond to watch them race; the frog and turtles, the turtles won; frogs by the pool now there's more, saying, *sign me up, sign me up*; new race has just begun, tomorrow at ten; who won, who won!!! Frogs by the pool.

Family is Everything

I'm stressing about helping my family; it's overwhelming; it's like they want me to cash out, they studying my stash route like I'm home alone. I'm fend to set it off Queen Latifa style; fuck it. They all wrong; run me here, do my hair, take me here; they don't care, trying to share the responsibility. That's silly. You see I live way over here, burning my gas. I'm a victim in this madness. I gotta grab this. I can't grasp this family shit; you can have it. Fuck the madness but I ain't even mad, shit, so I pick up the pieces like I'm doing the leases. I gots to release this bullshit real rips, spills sip, more shit. This is bullshit. I gots to get my grip right. I can't flip like yesterday's news; they put it on cruise control before they lose control. Oh oh oh, get up, don't shift a tear. I can't stop here. I'm stressing about helping my family. I'm sorry for the filthiness that's coming out of me. I'm stressing about my family. My pops ask if I want to go to the bar. I'm stressing about helping my family, family.

My nerves are bad. I need a penis so I smoke this shit and dream it; wait a minute. Pull over, y'all, just working to pay bills. I'm stressful, no caressing and make meals; can't chill. I'm stressful. can't even afford my rent, my lent. The sheets I lie on y'all play on; fuck a Plan B gotta go with Plan C so I can see y'all we raw, how you get more money than me and be broke. She said this is different shit; different strokes for different folks; y'all don't call me crazy, don't call me jazzman. I'm working on some shit that y'all can't stand; y'all my nerves are bad. I need a penis so I smoke this shit and dream it.

When I say spook, you say Halloween. I'm something like Tyler Perry. I wanna be scary ghost, and goblins don't come near me. When I say spook you say Halloween. Spook, I'ma let the dogs out; it's about to get haunted. You're going to scream *I don't want it*. There's a guy dressed up like Jason Myers, running me around the yard of my own house. I ran and I ran 'til I fell in a hole. I screamed, "Freddie Krueger is down here!" He threw me six feet in the air. I hit the trampoline and landed on the roof. Oh no, Jason Myers. I felt through the sky roof, bleeding. I limped around looking for safety. When Freddy Krueger saw me he ran off. thinking I was Jason Myers, so I hid in the basement. There was no more chasin'. When I say spook, you say Halloween; spook until the next season.

Just Because

Just because we take the same path doesn't mean we have the same values; just because we stare a certain way doesn't mean we're angry; just because we dress a certain way doesn't mean we're gangsters or whores; just because we talk this way doesn't mean we're dumb; just because the light's not on doesn't mean the bills are not paid; just because I say this, don't take this the wrong way, just because you cuss that way, that just means you're ugly.

I ain't mean enough, not fighting back, not talking up for one-self. I ain't mean enough, not standing my ground when things get tough. You gots to get tougher; sometimes even rougher. I ain't mean enough; they say if looks could kill I'd be for real; if only I had the angry look I'd be for real; the heavy voice that gives you the chills. I ain't mean enough, not fighting back, not talking up for oneself. I ain't mean enough.

Shotgun .357 Magnum

I ain't talking about a condom neither; he said when he fuck her he's going to leave her. I heard the gunshot two doors down; they found the body on the floor, the whore in the tour. Who would of thought it would be his last score? Drugs all over the place. Here's your case: he took her and her family and put them out, then took them back, never understanding it's a rap how things would unwrap, unfold; now all the bullshit stories being told. I gotta fold close your hands. I kneel to pray: dear God, please save the day. How can one man destroy a family? .357 shotgun, and I ain't talking condom, neither. I gotta fold close your hands. I kneel to pray: dear God, please save the day.

t's messed up when the military makes you forget your talents because of boundaries; you never found it. When the sounds hits all you know is blitz to get grips; don't fit; hungry as shit; where are my lifts? The gifts we don't give to live is to grieve. Who figures what's up their sleeves. My meds I need 'til the mission complete; military is needed, and we grieve it only when we leave it; the stories they left us, the families contest the trust that left us a mess, so I must cuss; where the fuck is my loved one, my only son, my only son? Nobody gives a fuck until the mission's completed; they don't give a fuck, the mission deleted; hold up repeated.

Too Much Life for Me to Escape

Never thought that I would say this y'all but I hate my Clucking Family, and I'm not talking about my immediate family, the ones who left me on this clucking tree swinging like a clucking leaf; this mental shit gots to go so I go harder every day. I'm in entrepreneur now. When they found me they said I have sound. I thought I was lost just to realize now how I can be a boss; lost souls forever. I'm bringing that cheddar, some shit we gots to treasure so here's my clucking letter, cluck the black and white ink, yo. I'ma increase the link, though I gots to make 'em think so when they blink, yo, I'ma make 'em hate me forever, though here's my clucking letter, yo; the cost to be beautiful. Now they're talking how they sucking the cuticle; too much of life for me to escape.

Nature

Sitting in the back yard I hear the birds singing, enjoying the peacefulness, taking a break from writing. I feel like Tarzan, I'm a monkey in the trees watching frogs by the ponds; it's all about me. My eyes are open. I can finally see nature, is just where I want to be. I see dolphins on the land like they are playing in the sand, caressing the man; snakes in the dirt like they are playing a band; stand up like man to give us a hand; mountains above me; the sky so lovely. Here are my hugs. See I'm loving the universe when I accept the fact it's not all about you; first the waters beneath us that make the sounds that found us, will never leave us from since the earth that found us; somehow it crowns us Nature.

Know Suicide

I just want to cry when I think about people who want to hurt themselves. I don't want to laugh just thinking about how I'm going to pass. They say laughter's good for the soul; sometimes I feel bold. I'm not talking about death when I mention passing in someone's life; let past that's been left. I turn right in my mind; it's bright. I don't want to laugh. I just want to pass but let past suicide missions. What's left inside a darkened side pass that you couldn't get past; let past suppressed feelings allow us not to eat. I'm hungry. No friends. I'm lonely. The cowardly act of the gun. Look, son, I don't care who's there; your mind's playing tricks on you to treat you like you're not number one or worth it. not here, you don't hear, pal. The gun went off, it don't care. I don't want to cry. I don't want to laugh just thinking about how I'm going to pass; let past. I'm not talking about death's pass, the past those thoughts of suicidal missions. I don't want to cry. I don't want to laugh just thinking about how I'm going to pass the past when I think about people doing suicidal missions. I cry; let past the past keep your mind clear, stay focused on everything that's positive; it's all possible. Let past the past of inside hurt pain that's so deep, so steep, can't reach beneath the pass; let past that's positive. It's possible very possible, extremely possible.

Crises When You Don't Pay Attention

They say before you leap, you leap, you may find yourself dealing with a creep. Is it even relevant? I ain't selling it, creepy; the least be everything; ain't always what it seem to be. Make a team and be drawn in and see it is very relevant; is he elegant, does he plan trips or just take 'em, does he obey laws or just break 'em, does he not communicate well with his family or escape them? A lot of things you can't tape themt. Something's haul to escape them; they say look before you leap; you can't tape them, then something is hard to escape them; they say look before you leap, you might find yourself dealing with a creep; if you treat this situation like leap year, you hardly care; they say look before you leap, you may find yourself dealing with a creep.

I Ain't No Doctor

I ain't no doctor, y'all, but stay on your meds. I'm thinking about someone who has a split personality. I can't imagine saying this but doing that, and this trauma from sexual or emotional abuse in you; feels like there's no outlet; let's not think about the bad memories. It's a mess on the systems of the body, like Ritalin revealing lithium, messing with logical thinking, unhealthy thinking. I ain't no doctor, y'all, but stay on your meds. I want to simplify with you but I can't get through. I only cried with you 'cause I can't get through; you only cried 'cause you didn't know what to do. Most of your friends ran away but I still stay with your mental; seems like it's slipping every day. with the where's my dog, have you seen my cat. Arguments for nothing like I'm fronting. I ain't no doctor, y'all, but stay on your meds. I'm thinking of someone who has a split personality.

Bullied

Imagine being a little boy or girl, like most kids trying to fit in, so you find yourself doing things that you wouldn't normally do, like sitting in a classroom, scared to speak up when the teacher ask you a question; you don't know, so fails you for the lesson; now you're teased the whole year through, being called a dummy, like what I do now? Insecurities set in, feelings like you can't win, so you pretend to fit in, scared to talk to the teachers, so you follow the crowds. Now you've lost your smile, your style. I won't pretend to be or care to see the other side of me; some would say I should mind my business, the cowardly act of others, but this world is our business on how we live and treat each other. I'd rather take this knife to myself, knowing it's bad for my health, dealing with being bullied never wins. Imagine being a little boy or girl, like most kids trying to fit in.

Priceless

It used to be a dollar for two, a dollar twenty-nine, make it do what it do, talking about working for the white man; it's not the white man, it's the right man; when life comes to a cost for all of us we must seek strength from one another; instead we rob strength from one another, don't teach one another until it's meaningless; they say if you look at the sky you would see the horizon; if you look in my eyes you would see that I'm crying, then try figuring out where is my mind is inside this nonsense, nonsense.

Matrimony

He asked for my hand in marriage, like he planned this holy matrimony; beautiful. Beauty beyond what I can see; secrets between us; the means of us I trust. The happiness we bring each other, some kind of lovers. The trials and challenges before us, who knows, only to grow in us. The climaxes between us keep the bond one union; stay tuned in some dreams we share; our dreams are shared between us; the house we built, the children we raised. To seal the deal he asked for my hand in marriage, like he plans this holy matrimony. I'm never lonely; he asked for my hand in marriage.

My God forget a clock, talkin' about the time and their rights; forget a clock. My time is my time. When I put this clock in your mouth, you gonna press rewind; put this clock in your house. I just read your mind, nothing in life seems ever on time. I'm getting cussed out 'cause evil wants to win. Looking out the window, they're saying, *blow me if you can.* My God said, *I give you until the end, stop clock, and roll twenty-two clocks in your mouth.* No pretend.

God Spoke to Me

One day I was on the road, thinking I swerved to pull over. A cop pulled up and said, "I have grounds to write you a ticket,"

I said, "God said pull over, I will take the wheel. I know the road you need to take. Hurry up, hit the brakes." If I could be God for one day, I say, "Come and take this walk with me in the desert for forty day and forty nights. I'd change your life."

I know one day you would like to get married instead of getting with these brothers that don't believe in carats, and I'm not talking vegetables. I know you're think things aren't going to change the second day, then on the third day God said, "Don't turn and be a crook"; the fourth day God said, "Stop and look"; the fifth day he said, "What you cooked?" the sixth day God said, "Work's still not done"; seventh day God said, "I gots to rest"; the eighth day God said, "You be best"; the ninth day God said to me, "Why are you stressed?"

The Tenth day I said, "God, I must confess, I'm a mess. How can I pass the test?"

The eleventh day God said, "I'ma leave you alone"; the twelfth day God said, "I knew you would figure out your wrongs." The thirteenth day we were singing songs. The fourteenth day God said, "One day we're all going to get along"; the fifteenth day He said, "I'm gone," but was never gone. The sixteenth day we were skipping along; the seventeenth day we went down by the Jordan River to get baptized into the body of Christ for the remission of sin and to conversate; the eighteenth day God said, "I can't tell you everything or show you." The nineteenth day God said, "I don't have time to play."

The twentieth day I said, "God, you have a wonderful sense of humor."

The twenty-first day God said to me, "You have my love; you will be fine the rest of the way. From days twenty-two to forty we journey until God returns again.

Never Assume

People assume all the time. as if that's normal. Well it's in old saying: you make an ass out of you and an ass out of me; getting caught up in this story of Adam's wife assumed the worst the independence was her being or him being themselves; independence was the act of the really a reality, audacity. People that assume cascade undermining, not indulging the situation, desperation; if you try being in an endeavor you self-scrutiny oneself. Don't assume, scrutinize.

False Reality

They say everything is not what it seems to be, but what if it's reality, or is it just a fantasy, like she's seeing something for the first time and got lost, was dressed to impress herself but left herself with the reality that wasn't there; her tears she cried; she cared, dealing with a military man for years; he jeered at times, at her bad stares, at times at her that left her scared to share the stories inside of her; they say everything is not what it seems to be, but what if reality is really a reality?

Realize

I live my life for my kids, never life for me never; realized he wasn't right for me. I'm sorry I was never right for you. Always talking 'bout your wife, and you never realized it was the price in two. I'ma put my emotions in this song; why they always in the wrong? You wouldn't know a diamond if it jumped off your plate. A name like LP Baby. I'm hard to erase. I'm sorry I wasn't right for you, always talking 'bout your wife and you never realized it was the price in two. Well my life's not through. I lived my life for my kids, never life for me never; realized he wasn't right for me/ I ain't losin'. Every day I'm cruisin'. I stay it's you who's losing.

Feelings

You ever wake up in the morning feeling like today is not a good day. Just feeling crappy, not cranky, *crappy*, as the day goes on. If I don't pull myself together I'ma stay cranky. My sons are home. Good news from boot camp, and I've heard my daughter is getting kicked out of her friend's home. Due to finances. Now I'm starting to get cranky. My mind's all over the place; I can't think. But hell. Hell is here; forget all that talk about being parents of the year. Now I'm trying to save my dare. My dare: pull yourself together, my mother would say. And get over here. This is an issue that will get addressed. This is like being raped in a song. This is gonna take all night long. You ever wake up in the morning feeling like today is not a good day. Just feeling crappy, not cranky, *crappy*. But you get through the day. At the end you have your way. Because you get up and out. Business-wise you're on your way; you can't rush progress. Don't cut your nose off to spite your face.

Lost Hope

The things we do to destroy hope I'ma start with relationships that went too long and never congregated, left to tell this song, a daughter or son witnessing a mother on drugs; he or she shrugged on emotions, someone doing everything for you, not being mindful thinking they helpful. Almost always leave you feeling hopeless. Don't stroke this but I stroked it, getting the life choked out of you, then when they lie to you, being raped in a thong. I can keep telling these stories all night long but I don't want to leave you hopeless, so I stroked it when I stroked this. I'm the butterfly poet. Have you walked around looking like Pinocchio; you bound to grow it. Lost hope, no lost hope; here, get up; you know it. Leona Peace

*Y*ou ever walked around with a complexes 'cause somebody treated you bad; now you think that's all grandy and sad, thinking about the color of our skin, the way we dress, do I fit in. Complex. Too much makeup to shape up; grape is the flavor now. Shape up; your drape sucks. Complexes. The fake us; you ever had a man treat you like he's Bob the Builder? It's like a metaphor how they get you up to let you down; he said he slaughtered the chick, man; he had to kill her talking 'bout her dreams. He screamed. The complex he feens the mcans to dream perceptions and wished in response to the threat to the stability of thy self-complexed rioting of your health.

Failures

I was a failure since I've started school; always passed with a D 'cause I was always chasing the dongs while the guys chase the thongs. I never wanted to do my homework, failures each class. I was way gone, just wronged. The times I've tried to shine, like painting class when I drew a unique pyramid, then paint fell and destroyed the scenery; wasn't a total failure; the pyramid was still there. Failures. Always late for school, never completed assignments, drinking, and don't quit; failure happens; too soon destroys and loom; so make your tunes like they say; if you make your bed you got to lie in it. Watch how you start your journey in life; don't be a failure and pay the price. Failure.

now communication, thinking, What's worse, you finding out information on the internet that someone in your family passed away or in person? Some of y'all lie to strangers; lie in things even stranger; you lie in your sleep, no communicating; know like it's hard to speak. Communication is what I seek so I speak to release my anger, even stranger; you lie lies and things, no communication, no communication; know.

Environment

The music we listen to messes up the environment; the foods we grow are cheap, but don't know; the movies we teach you, how to deceive you, the things you believe; it's like it's way beneath you, not getting the facts too; it's black and can't see though now. I can't trace you, trying to erase you; it's not a witch hunt. I'm blunt like a stunt. I'm just trying to reach you, each of you. Every one of you. I'm not through the environment; the choices we make, the mistakes. I won't take I see the world as great this world; we can't escape, looking for a place to belong to. Here's our song; shoot ally hoop. I'ma bring this song like Picasso so you can be fascinated we can save the environment if imagined.

They say real Gs move in silence, not with the violence that keep us hollering, the wise should lead the way. Words they need, they give the structure to please everybody, leaving no knots to untie. United we ride to glide. The silence is too high. Leads us to destruction and I can't stand for real Gs that move in silence. So I untie the knots they leave inside to believe that we should be left to cry. Let your voices be heard; the wise lead to bring structures and peace in case we gain; no pain remains. They say real Gs move in silence; I say wisdome is to be let your voices be heard.

It's okay to not be okay. We walk around and hide what's really going on inside. The slide cry, the slide why. The slide high. Why I had to act strong trying to shield my kids from what's really going wrong with me. My song they may not see. We cry and we have borderline personalities. Wanting someone to agree just because. Doesn't make matters right hiding the truth inside of me. We grown but we still need to elaborate. Collaborate the slide cry. We will see what's going on inside of me. I was drinking every day to suppress my pain, can't sleep. I prayed to God. Dear God, I know you hear me; please take this pain from inside of me. It's okay to not be okay. As long as I was moving I'm good. When I stopped I had to deal with it. Learning to understand my pain. Thank God it's okay to not be okay; there were nights I couldn't sleep, wanted to make myself cry just for my body to shut down and go to sleep. It's okay to not be okay; we will get through it. It's okay to not be okay.

Invisible Man

Imagine trying that door and no one is there, invisible. Imagine being in a relationship, feeling like you're all alone, your man's home but visually gone. Terrance Hayes. I admire his song, stories; stories are inevitable to not acknowledge; it is inevitable. Invisible man. I don't know slow to grow some circumstances at hand that are invisible, like when MB Dribble or not knowing what someone is going through, invisible, like a shadow to be free; his fear was inevitable when he went to save the lady on the roof when he heard her hollering. I'm going to be with my dad to be invisible, invisible.

Sorry

Sorry for the things I've said; sorry for the things I've read; sorry about the ways I've acted and shouldn't have done. Sorry about the ways I've cussed you out and I've should have said sorry. Sorry about the way I behaved in the bed. Sorry about the times things just weren't fair. Sorry about the time you walked through the storms; that's the time you should've been warned. You ever wake up in the morning feeling sorry for yourselves? I'm sorry about the times I just wasn't me, sorry. Tired of saying sorry; sorry, you see.

$\mathcal{F}$eel you, she says 'til you tell him to marry you; they don't carry you, feel you, is it the real you? Killing us softly, awful feel you do. I trust you will you marry me, feel you; she says 'til you tell him off, lost you, will you marry me? Carry me. It's scary. See, feel you, she says, until she never heard you feel you; she says feel you; in other words make sure you feel you before you marry him marry you. I'm not trying to capture no hearts, feel you; she says until you tell him to marry you, getting married for all the wrong reasons is it the real you feel you; she says feel you.

How can I see when you cover my eyes? I know you got a vision but what you want me to see remains about the way we used to be, like when we kissed under the tree. How can I see when you cover my eyes? You bought me diamond rings, and I felt free. I remain how you held me so tight. How can I see when you cover my eyes? It's like you're blocking my light; don't trip me up when you rub me down; we make it right. How can I see when you cover my eyes? I'm like beauty and the beast. How can I see when you cover my eyes? You can't replace a man's love in the home. How can I see when you cover my eyes? We just need some substance in our life and time to be alone. How can one be blinded by the choices someone else makes? Balance is in the sacrifice. How can I see when you cover my eyes?

Strange

You ever hear someone say to you they heard a cat piss on a dog? Strange people say things all the time that don't make sense. Strange, no change, trying to read facial expressions; strange body chemistry might be strange, seeing something you never saw before; strange, going to unfamiliar places, being around people who aren't positive, also people who shop in pajamas. Strange when someone doesn't agree with you; strange. I was told I am strange because they don't understand my personality; strange like someone sitting in a dark room all alone, someone might think that's strange.

he gifts God gives us we take for granted, like the air we breathe, the trees we see, the luxuries he gives, the religion we need, the relief, intrigue to believe there's no need; for what God set the Earth forth for; believe the cherries that grow, the birds that fly, the water that flows; my mind won't let go his every words flow. The ascent of my being. The blind that's not seeing. Just try believing. Even though we're grieving. The gifts God gives us. The dirt we walk on. The soil beneath us. They spoil and don't see. It toils me 'til it's coiled me to pieces.

Imagine

Imagine is the name of this poem. Imagine being broken 'cause the color of your skin. Imagine being chosen but don't not knowing where to begin. Imagine being frozen; we call that pretend. Imagine not voting; don't want to start over again. Imagine new life being born again, denied access. Imagine again. Imagine being lost, not knowing your identity. I was told I belonged to the Kennedys. Imagine being broken. Don't know what to begin imagining.

J asked God to put the sun in his shoe 'cause the sun glare was bothering me; he said, *you think I walk around and I don't know what to do. I walk this whole earth just to make sure nobody hurts.* They say people speak in tongues; when I hear that I wanna run 'cause I know I'm not right. I gotta go to church so I can got the Holy Ghost. God said, *child, keep doing the most; the Devil comes in many forms.* God said for me to stay in the pew, *you will keep warm,* meaning safe; you know what I told you to do, a reading from the second book of Maccabees; it happened that seven brothers with their mother were arrested and tortured with whips and scourges by the king. I'm like the last one in this story, not willing to sacrifice the laws of my ancestors. They jeered at Christ, the saying he's the chosen one; y'all stop saying I'm the chosen one; all are chosen but only a few make it into the kingdom of heaven. You ever hear people say I am talking to God and he's not answering back? That's because you haven't been paying attention. I asked God to put the sun in his shoe because the sun glare was bothering me; he said, *you think I walk this earth and I don't know you.*

f I told you I can move mountains you would say that I'm God, he used the spirit in using water. I never tried the spirit is. I just want to share it. The quiz is, do you test the times of the minds or do you line them up and go blind? Let's not underestimate the power of God; he said, *I am that I am.* I'm not am that I am. I am who I am because of God's visions of the unknown, the throne, no clones, my main bones drawn to the pain alone; society's mysteries keep kissing me. I'm like a cocoon when I step in the room; can be here today and gone tomorrow like the dust in yesterday's wind; if I told you I can move mountains you would say that I'm God; he used the spirit in using water. I never tried the spirit is.

My story of the phenomenal woman; she's like a plant that constantly grows the nourishments that bring pleasures in her strengths, her personality; she's different. Every one of us not laxing in an area of life, not relaxing to become what she was created for; a mind that builds like a man, that builds buildings and sometimes with her hands, not putting women down but building them up. Phenomenal woman, her essence, her eccentric meaning being creative, her smell, her touch, the mold that holds the earth together; her worth is priceless; my story of the phenomenal woman.

took hate and didn't let it consume me. I grew with the tunes. God said I'm on borrowed time; he took my heart. I said, *give it back*; he said, *not until the end of time*. I said, *that is whack*. How are people talking about how they love me when they slugged me, tugging, no hugging. What God already knew; he said, *you can beat the charge*. Don't cross it; take it to the Lord. I don't floss it, I'm talking to my Lord; just wanna say thank you, Jesus, for every season that you give me. God tells us *don't be scared when trials are tough*. I said, *how? I know you not going to get tired of me*. He said, *I know your mind and got your heart, so you can't even start fits*. You get kicked with the cross kick; just wanna relieve all my stress. Right now is a test, right row my sins are covered being in the church at the pew. God said *you thought you were through; just follow me and you will get some insight, the invite*. Beauty is in the eye of the beholder so I don't fold her. I let my light shine when is not bright; signs gotta follow Jesus, number one. please, God, take my mind where you want it to go, like the wintertime when you direct the snow. My friends said if he gets the mind then the ass would follow; his mind is hollow so I'ma pray for him through this song; gotta follow Jesus, number one. Please ah Hal' a Lu yah Hal' a Lu yah.

It's not like I want him to take me in his arms and embrace me when he doesn't know what chases me. The race be love, not to understand, underestimates me, pushing me around because he has no plans. No let on how to get out of a struggling situation. Juggling jobs that don't pay off. Trying to make sales on a ocky stand shop and plan government shutdown; families not around, drowning in the sounds of being broke, getting choked; now I'm provoked for the unnecessary uncertain undeserved it's not like I want him to take me in his arms and embrace me when he doesn't know what chases me; you can run but you can't hide

If it's tantalizing, then you're playing to when then you're playing with sin, Sugar free, is this really happening to me? I just don't have much time to watch things rot; you plot too much friction in the space between. Sometimes a lie is the best thing to more sad stories, tantalizing love is blind. Can't see your desire, saying it's all about the hustle but no muscle, tantalizing me, fatal attractions will show, tantalizing. I don't need a brother that I can use and abuse, taking me and then putting me out, tantalizing. When they threw me a curveball I threw it back, never ending, so tantalizing.

 ife goes on long offer the thrill of living is gone. Depends on how you look at life. Some drink for the thrill, some smoke, some kill, some people just looking for a thrill like a roller coaster. Just because you're wealthy doesn't mean you're thrilled to live in this life. Like after driving the fastest car, life goes on long after the thrill of living is gone. Some walk around and are already gone, dead due to the circumstances they are going through. Are you really looking at life? Did you pay the price? Life goes on long after the thrill of living is gone. Some say they've lived well. Did you really live? Life goes on long after the thrill of living is gone.

stroke sarre toil some people just looking for a thrill. Fight a roller coaster just because your wealthy doesn't n-can your bled to life in the lie Ake alter driving the fastest ear I goes on lott Wier the thrill of 5vit is gore .sore wall armed and is already gar dead due to the ciCUIMINCCS dry are going through= youreally lookigai YE did rupay the price life grres on long alter the thol of living ts gone so= say they'$e liked well did you really he loc goes on long after the thrill of living is gone